The Salem
Witch Trials

The Salem Witch Trials

Judith Bloom Fradin
Dennis Brindell Fradin

 **Marshall Cavendish**
Benchmark
New York

Marshall Cavendish Benchmark
99 White Plains Road
Tarrytown, New York 10591-5502
www.marshallcavendish.us

All Internet sites were available and accurate when sent to press.

Library of Congress Cataloging-in-Publication Data
Fradin, Judith Bloom.
The Salem witch trials / by Judith Bloom Fradin & Dennis Brindell Fradin.
p. cm. — (Turning points in U.S. history)
Summary: "Covers the Salem Witch Trials as a watershed event in U.S. history, influencing social, economic, and political policies
that shaped the nation's future"—Provided by publisher.
Includes bibliographical references and index.
ISBN 978-0-7614-3013-1
1. Trials (Witchcraft)—Massachusetts—Salem—Juvenile literature.
2. Witchcraft—Massachusetts—Salem—History—Juvenile literature.
3. Salem (Mass.)—Social conditions—Juvenile literature. I. Fradin, Dennis B. II.
Title.
KFM2478.8.W5F7 2009
133.4'3097445—dc22
2007037606

Photo research by Connie Gardner
Cover photo: Bettmann/CORBIS
Title Page: *Corbis:* Lee Snider/PhotoImages

The photographs in this book are used by permission and through the courtesy of: Francis G. Mayer, 6; Poodles Rock, 9; *Getty Images:* Hulton Archive, 10;
North Wind Picture Archives: 8, 16, 22, 26; *The Image Works:* Charles Walker Topham, 12; Arena Pal/Topham, 30; Charles Walker, Topfoto, 36; *Alamy:* North
Wind Picture Archives, 20, 28; *Bridgeman Art Library:* Samuel Parris, c 1865 (oil on card) by American School (17th century) c Massachusetts Historical
Society, Boston, MA, USA, 19; Witchcraft Victims on the way to the Gallows, illustration in the 'Boston Herald', published 14th May 1930 (colour litho) by
Frederick Coffay Yohn (1875-1933) (after) c Peabody Essex Museum, Salem, Massachusetts, USA, 32, 42-43; Increase Mather (1639-1723) 1688 (oil on can-
vas) by or Spriett Spriet, jan van der (b. 1700), 35.

Editor: Deborah Grahame
Publisher: Michelle Bisson
Art Director: Anahid Hamparian

Printed in Malaysia
3 5 6 4 2

Contents

The Witch of Endor, mentioned in the Old Testament of the Bible, brings forth the prophet Samuel's ghost with dire news for King Saul.

CHAPTER ONE

Witchcraft in the Old World

People have believed in witches for thousands of years. *The Odyssey*, a story dating back 2,700 years, featured a witch. Her name was Circe, and she turned men into pigs. The Bible also talks about witchcraft. The Old Testament's book of Exodus states, "Thou shalt not suffer a witch to live."

Over the centuries, people around the world have had various ideas about witchcraft. Europeans believed that witches were mainly women. People thought witches made deals with God's wicked enemy, known as the devil or Satan. The devil supposedly gave witches money, land, or

Sorcerers, also known as witches, are shown practicing rituals in a ring of fire surrounded by eerie symbols of their mysterious art.

other valuable gifts. In return, the witch had to help the devil with his evil work. This often meant harming people by **supernatural** means.

People claimed that witches caused accidents and made people become ill. Witches were blamed for killing crops and livestock, creating bad weather, and killing babies. They were thought to do harm by saying magic words, which was called casting a spell. Just by looking at people with her **evil eye**, it was said, a witch could injure them.

Witches were said to have other supernatural powers. A magic ointment enabled them to fly. They could also fly around on poles or broomsticks. Witches could make themselves invisible or change into animals such as cats, wolves, and mice.

People invented ways to tell if someone was a witch. Supposedly witches had odd moles and birthmarks on their bodies called witches' marks. If asked to recite the Lord's Prayer, a witch could not do it without stumbling over the words.

This early twentieth-century Halloween postcard features a fanciful image of a flying witch.

Centuries ago, crowds gathered in public squares throughout Europe to witness and even cheer the execution of people condemned for practicing witchcraft.

A witch could also send out her **specter**—a kind of ghost—to do her wicked deeds. If someone saw a specter of a particular person, it was said, that person must be a witch.

Accusing people of being witches was an easy way to attack enemies. It was also a way to punish people who were seen as different. For example, families that grew better crops than their neighbors might be accused of being witches. People often accused their neighbors who did not attend church. In Europe between the 1400s and the 1600s, huge numbers of people were **persecuted** as witches. Often people **tortured** them to make them confess to witchcraft or to name other witches. According to some estimates, 30,000 Europeans were put to death for being witches. About three-fourths of the victims were women. Others estimate that more than a million so-called witches were hanged or burned.

King of Scotland James VI, who later became James I of England, oversees the beating of accused witches in this 1590 woodcut.

CHAPTER TWO

Witches in the New World

In the 1600s most Europeans still believed in witches. King James I's Witchcraft Act became law in 1604. The law made practicing any kind of witchcraft a crime punishable by hanging. Witchcraft trials were held in England throughout the 1600s. Periods when many accusations were made became known as witch hunts. During a witch hunt from 1645 to 1647, several hundred English people were hanged for being witches.

Meanwhile, English people colonized North America starting in the early 1600s. The first English colony, Virginia, was settled in 1607. Next came Massachusetts, which was colonized in 1620. The English then settled in eleven other American colonies.

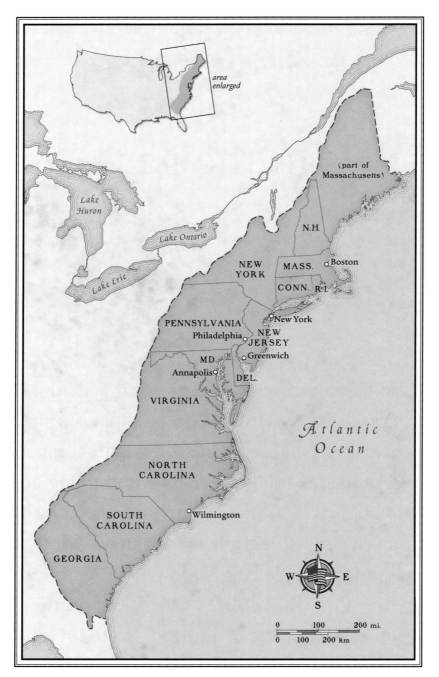

The original thirteen American colonies were settled between 1607 and 1733.

Just as in England, some colonists were accused of being witches. A Massachusetts woman named Margaret Jones argued with some of her neighbors. Soon after the argument, the neighbors' farm animals became ill or died. The neighbors accused Margaret Jones of **bewitching** their animals. Jones was put to death in 1648. She was the first accused witch in Massachusetts to be **executed**.

The Margaret Jones execution was part of a witch hunt that lasted from 1647 to 1663 throughout New England. During those years, about eighty New Englanders were accused of practicing witchcraft. Fifteen were put to death, and all but two were women. However, the biggest witch hunt in American history was yet to come.

Executed or Murdered?

We say witches were *executed* because authorities put them to death according to laws of the time. By modern standards, though, the so-called witches were not executed. They were murdered. None of them had the evil powers they were accused of having. In addition, they were denied a fair chance to defend themselves.

Puritans, who established the settlement of Plymouth in 1620, worshiping together in simple surroundings.

CHAPTER THREE

The Witch Scare Begins at Salem

Many of the colonists in Massachusetts were Christian people called Puritans. The Puritans wanted to purify, or improve, religion by simplifying services and focusing on the Bible. Puritans founded Salem, Massachusetts, in 1628. They established Boston two years later.

By the 1690s Salem was home to a few hundred families. It was divided into two sections. Salem Town was a business center and fishing port. Salem Village was composed of scattered farms within several miles of Salem Town. When discussing the Salem witch crisis, people today usually refer to the two sections together as Salem.

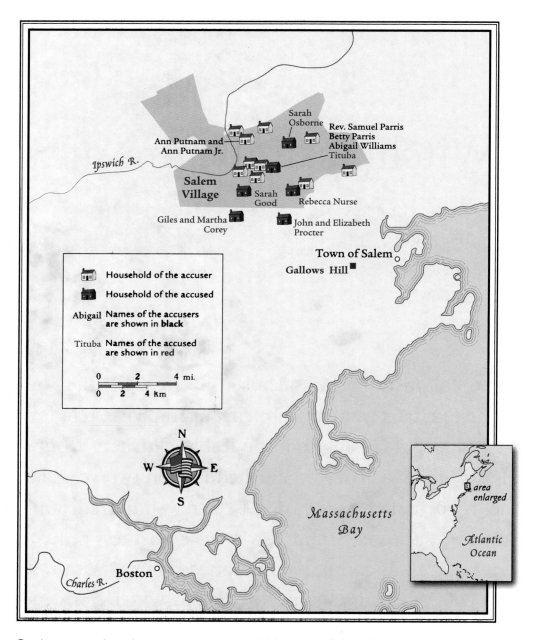

Both accused and accusers were neighbors in Salem Village—and in some cases, such as the Parrises', even lived in the same household.

The witch trouble began in early 1692 in Reverend Samuel Parris's home in Salem Village. Reverend Parris and his wife had a nine-year-old daughter, Betty. The Parrises were also raising Betty's eleven-year-old cousin, Abigail Williams. Betty and Abigail became bored that winter. To pass the time, the cousins played a game. They poured an egg white into a glass of water. According to the girls, the shape that the egg white formed was a clue about a girl's future husband. For example, if the egg white formed the shape of a ship, it meant the girl would marry a sailor.

Samuel Parris (1653–1720)

The first egg white took the shape of a coffin. The girls were scared. A coffin was a container for burying the dead. Was this a hint that death and disaster were about to happen?

Soon after they played their game, the girls began having what were called fits. Their bodies twisted into odd positions, as if invisible forces were attacking the girls. They choked, as if unseen hands clutched their

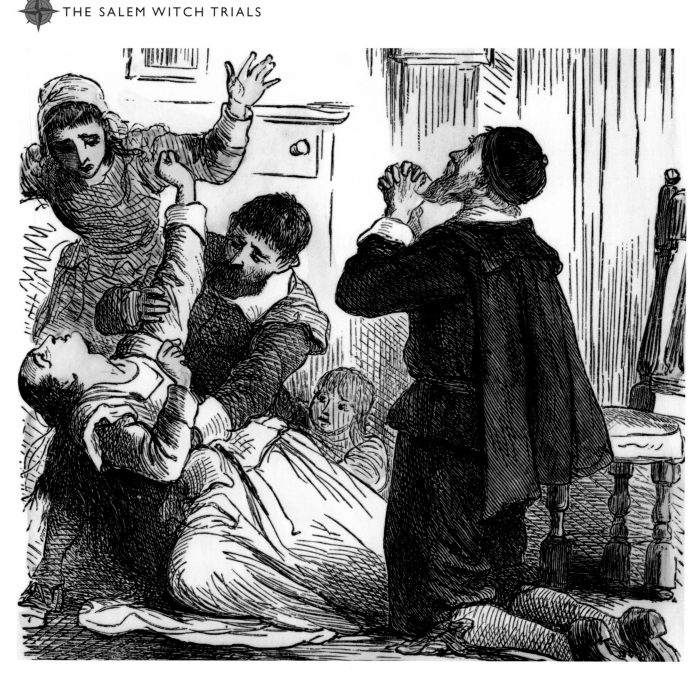

Terrified families of Salem Village summoned ministers and doctors to help them deal with the mad ravings of their daughters.

throats. They screamed that they were being bitten and pinched. The girls made strange animal noises. They flapped their arms, as if they were trying to fly.

Word about Betty and Abigail's fits spread throughout Salem. Neighbor girls and women began to have similar attacks. Among the new victims were Ann Putnam and her twelve-year-old daughter, Ann Putnam Jr. Meanwhile, doctors were called in to determine what ailed Betty Parris and Abigail Williams. Dr. William Griggs had the answer: "The evil hand is upon them. The girls are victims of witchcraft!"

To rid New England of so-called witches, town leaders arrested people they considered outside society—especially older women who seemed physically ugly or strange in some way.

CHAPTER FOUR

The Salem Witch Hunt

Reverend Parris ordered his daughter and niece to name who was bewitching them. Betty, Abigail, and other girls gave three names. One was Tituba, a slave in the Parris home. Another was Sarah Good, a beggar who argued with people if they did not give her food. The third, Sarah Osborne, was the subject of gossip because she had married her servant after her first husband died. The three **suspects** were arrested on February 29, 1692. This began what is known as the Salem witch hunt.

Town leaders questioned the three women. Good and Osborne **denied** that they were witches. As a slave, Tituba was used to telling white people what they wanted to hear. She confessed to being a witch.

Who Was Tituba?

Tituba is a mysterious figure in the Salem witchcraft story. We do not know when she was born. We are not sure where she was from, either. Many historians say Tituba was a Native American. Others think she was of African origin. She became Samuel Parris's slave when he lived on the Caribbean island of Barbados. When Parris moved to Massachusetts in 1680, he brought Tituba and a slave named John Indian with him. In 1689—about the time that the Parrises settled in Salem—Tituba married Indian. Tituba reportedly had one child, a daughter named Violet.

Tituba was the first person to be accused in the Salem witch hunt. She was also the first to confess to being a witch. It is believed that Reverend Parris made Tituba confess by beating her. Later Tituba said she was not a witch after all.

Reverend Parris was angry with Tituba for taking back her confession. He would not pay the fee to get her out of jail. She had to spend more than a year imprisoned. She was not released until an unknown person paid her jail fee and bought her. What happened to Tituba after her release also remains a mystery.

"The Devil came to me and bid me serve him," she said. Tituba added that there were many other witches in the area, including Good and Osborne. The three women were jailed to await trial for practicing witchcraft.

In 1692 most colonists believed in witchcraft. The news that witches had filled the area was alarming. Panic raced through Salem. From there it spread to Andover and other eastern Massachusetts towns. People spoke, wrote, and even dreamed about witches. They accused people they knew of being witches. Ann Putnam Jr. alone accused sixty-two individuals of practicing witchcraft.

It was easy to claim that people were witches. Did someone have an unusual scar? It must be a witch's mark. Did the night shadows in a bedroom resemble someone's face? It must be a witch's specter. Did a person have a coughing fit whenever a neighbor came into view? That neighbor must be a witch casting a spell. Over a period of several months, hundreds of people in and near Salem were accused of witchcraft. About two hundred were imprisoned.

The first three accused witches were people of low social standing. As time passed, however, the group of accused witches included respected citizens. Rebecca Nurse, John and Elizabeth Proctor, and Reverend George Burroughs were prime examples.

Rebecca Nurse was a seventy-one-year-old mother and grandmother. She was known around Salem for her kindness and fine character. In March 1692 Ann Putnam and Ann Putnam Jr. claimed that Nurse's specter had attacked them. Some people suspected that the Putnams were striking back at Rebecca because the two families had argued over

These are the written remarks of men who interviewed Ann Putnam and her daughter on May 31, 1692.

land. Nurse was arrested and jailed. Her sisters, Mary Easty and Sarah Cloyce, were also arrested on suspicion of practicing witchcraft.

John and Elizabeth Proctor were a well-off couple who owned a tavern and a large farm. John was one of few people who openly criticized the witch hunt. In his opinion the accusers were making up stories about witches. On March 25, 1692—the day after Rebecca Nurse was jailed—Proctor made angry comments in a tavern. Unless the witch hunt stopped, he said, "We should all be witches." He added that the accusers were the ones who should be punished. Soon afterward, Abigail Williams said that John and Elizabeth Proctor's specters had pinched her. The Proctors were accused of witchcraft and jailed.

George Burroughs was a minister who had served at the Puritan church in Salem Village. Reverend Burroughs's **congregation** disliked him. They had not paid him his salary, so he had quit and moved to Maine. In spring of 1692, several Salem-area people claimed they had seen Reverend Burroughs's specter leading witches' meetings. Burroughs was arrested in Maine. He was taken back to Salem and jailed as another accused witch.

By late spring in 1692, the jails in Salem and nearby areas were filled to overflowing with accused witches. What would happen to them?

The girls' strange behavior continued during the Salem witch trials and often disrupted the proceedings.

CHAPTER FIVE

The Salem Witch Trials

The trials of the accused witches began on June 2, 1692. The Salem witch trials were not what we would call fair. The accused were not defended by lawyers. Some of the victims avoided trial by confessing their guilt and agreeing to **testify** against other accused witches. In the end, the people placed on trial were mainly those who continued to deny being witches. To save their necks, many confessed witches made up stories to help **convict** those placed on trial. John Proctor summed up the situation in a letter. The judges and jury "**condemned** us already before our trials," he wrote.

A woman named Bridget Bishop was the first person to be tried. A neighboring farm couple accused Bishop of bewitching their hog. They

claimed she had made the animal go deaf and blind. Bishop was found guilty of practicing witchcraft. She was sentenced to be hanged.

Rebecca Nurse's trial was held on June 29. A widow accused Rebecca of killing her husband by casting a spell on him three years earlier.

Telling the Story

There are many stories, movies, books, and plays relating to the Salem witch hunt and trials. The most famous of these works is *The Crucible*, a 1952 play by Arthur Miller. Although the characters in Miller's play are actual people, *The Crucible* is a fictionalized (not completely true or factual) account of what happened in Salem. Robert Ward's 1961 opera, also called *The Crucible*, is based on Miller's play. The opera won the 1962 Pulitzer Prize for Music.

This scene from a 1998 production of the play *The Crucible* shows several women reacting to being supposedly pinched and pricked supernaturally by the witches on trial.

Another woman testified that Nurse's specter was sticking her with pins right in court. She had a bloody knee to prove it. However, the woman had been seen jabbing herself with pins. The jury found Rebecca not guilty of witchcraft. One of the judges called the **verdict** unacceptable. The jury reconsidered and came back with a new verdict: guilty. Nurse was sentenced to be hanged. Sarah Good and three other women were given the same sentence in late June.

George Burroughs was tried on August 5. Because he was a minister and was thought to be the witches' leader, his trial drew a large crowd. Eight confessed witches testified that Burroughs had **lured** them into witchcraft. Nine people testified that Burroughs was supernaturally strong for a small man. Once he had lifted a barrel of molasses by himself. People felt that only the devil could have given him such strength. Reverend Burroughs was found guilty of practicing witchcraft with a sentence of hanging.

John and Elizabeth Proctor also were tried in early August. Several people testified that the couple's specters had tortured them. Even though twenty people had signed a **petition** saying that the Proctors were not witches, the jury found the Proctors guilty. They, too, were sentenced to be hanged. Because Elizabeth Proctor was pregnant, the court decided to let her live until after she had her baby.

This painting, created in 1930 and displayed in a museum in Salem today, depicts people condemned to be executed as they are led to the gallows amid the chaos of the crowds.

CHAPTER SIX

Executions—
and the Madness Ends

Between June and September 1692, nineteen people were hanged in Salem for practicing witchcraft. Crowds came to see the hangings and to hear the condemned witches' last words.

Bridget Bishop was executed first. She claimed innocence to the end. Bishop was hanged on June 10.

Rebecca Nurse, Susanna Martin, Elizabeth Howe, Sarah Good, and Sarah Wildes were hanged on July 19. At the **gallows**, a minister urged Nurse to admit her guilt. "You are a liar!" Nurse shot back. "I am no more a witch than you are a **wizard**!" Minutes later, Nurse and the four other women were dead.

The hangings of George Burroughs, Martha Carrier, John Willard, George Jacobs Sr., and John Proctor happened on August 19. As his last act, Reverend Burroughs recited the Lord's Prayer perfectly. This disturbed the crowd, for supposedly witches could not recite the Lord's Prayer without making a mistake. Sitting on horseback, prominent Boston minister Cotton Mather tried to calm the onlookers. Reverend Mather told them that the devil must have helped Burroughs recite the Lord's Prayer correctly.

Eight more people were hanged on September 22. They were Rebecca Nurse's sister Mary Easty, Alice Parker, Ann Pudeator, Martha Corey, Margaret Scott, Wilmot Read, Mary Parker, and Samuel Wardwell. As they faced the hangman's noose, none of the victims would admit to being a witch.

There was a twentieth execution, but it was not a hanging. At his hearing, Giles Corey, a farmer and the husband of Martha Corey, refused to speak. He would not say whether he was or was not a witch. To try to force him to talk, authorities made him lie down and placed heavy rocks on him. Corey died in silence, crushed to death by the rocks.

People were not the only victims of the Salem witch hunt. Two dogs accused of witchcraft were also executed.

By fall of 1692, prominent people were being accused of witchcraft. For example, Mary Phips was accused of being a witch. She was the wife of William Phips, the governor of Massachusetts. A growing number of ministers and other leaders spoke out against the witch hunt and trials. They included Reverend Increase Mather, Cotton Mather's father. In October Increase Mather wrote, "It were better that Ten Suspected Witches should escape, than that one Innocent Person should be Condemned."

Governor Phips decided to end the madness. In late October 1692 he ordered that no further arrests of accused witches be made. Under Governor Phips's direction, the remaining so-called witches were released from jail in late 1692 and in 1693.

In the end the toll was much higher than twenty people.

Cotton Mather (1663–1728)

Father and Son Ministers: Increase and Cotton Mather

Increase Mather was born in Dorchester, Massachusetts. After graduating from Harvard College at age seventeen, he became a Puritan minister. Reverend Mather served at a Boston church for fifty-nine years. During that time he also served as president of Harvard College for sixteen years.

Increase Mather
(1639–1723)

Increase opposed the Salem witch trials. His essay, "Cases of Conscience Concerning Evil Spirits," published in fall of 1692, helped end the persecution of witches around Salem. Increase was married twice and had ten children. He lived to the age of eighty-four— quite a long life for colonial times.

Born in Boston, Cotton Mather was Increase's oldest child. Cotton graduated from Harvard when he was only fifteen. He later served as a minister at his father's church in Boston.

Cotton became the most famous of all Puritan ministers. He wrote hundreds of books. He was also one of the main supporters of the witch trials. In a sermon he praised the hanging of witches: "Some of the Witch Gang have been fairly Executed." Cotton was married three times and had fifteen children. He died one day after his sixty-fifth birthday.

Another Witch Hunt

To this day, when groups of people are persecuted, we often say a witch hunt is going on. During the 1950s, the lives and careers of many Americans were ruined when they were accused of being communists. (Communism was the form of government of the Soviet Union, a country that most Americans saw as an enemy at the time.) This shameful episode is often called a witch hunt.

Several people died while in prison. Also, many people's lives were ruined.

Historians disagree about where the blame lies for the Salem witch hunt and trials. Some say that **mass hysteria** gripped the Salem area. That is, people became so nervous and upset about witches that they could not think straight. Some people blame the girls who made the first accusations. They say the girls pretended to be bewitched just to get attention and feel important. Others blame the adults who used the witch scare to attack their enemies. Yet others blame Cotton Mather and Samuel Parris for encouraging the witch hunt.

There is also an unusual **theory** about the Salem witch hunt. Some scholars claim that Salem-area people ate bread that was infected by

Life After the Trials

What became of people involved in the Salem witch hunt and trials?

Relatives of Rebecca Nurse and other executed "witches" forced Reverend Samuel Parris to leave Salem in 1697. Parris settled with his family in Sudbury, Massachusetts, where he died in 1720.

Betty Parris married a Sudbury man. She had five children and lived to the age of about seventy-seven.

What became of Abigail Williams is unknown.

Ann Putnam Sr. died in 1699, a few years after the Salem witch trials. After her parents both died in 1699, Ann Putnam Jr. raised her nine younger brothers and sisters. In 1706 Ann made a public apology in the Salem Village church for her role in the witch hunt. She said she had come to believe the accused witches had been innocent.

Sarah Osborne died in jail in spring of 1692 while awaiting trial. Elizabeth Proctor gave birth to her baby in Salem's prison in early 1693. Elizabeth was among those released under Governor Phips's direction. By delaying her execution, her baby (who may not have survived infancy) had saved Elizabeth's life.

Sarah Cloyce, sister of Rebecca Nurse, was also among those released from prison. She returned to her family, but details of her later life are unknown.

ergot. These fungi can cause people who eat them to have hallucinations, or to see things that are not really there. Supporters of this theory say that Salem residents thought they saw witches flying and turning into animals because they suffered from ergot poisoning.

The Salem witch crisis was a turning point in U.S. history. When the nation's founders established the framework of the U.S. government in the late 1700s, they were aware of the many injustices of colonial times. These included the Salem witch hunt and trials. The founders included basic protections for Americans in the Bill of Rights, which took effect in 1791. For example, Americans accused of crimes have the right to a fair trial "by an **impartial** jury." With this kind of protection, it was hoped that what happened in Salem in 1692 would never be repeated.

Glossary

bewitching—Casting a spell upon someone.

condemned—Pronounced guilty; about to be punished.

congregation—A group of people who meet for religious services.

convict—To prove guilty.

denied—Declared untrue.

evil eye—Causing harm by merely glaring at someone.

executed—Killed as a legal punishment.

gallows—A device for hanging people.

impartial—Fair; not favoring one side of an argument or issue.

lured—Tempted.

mass hysteria—A condition in which many people in a community become so upset that they cannot think straight.

persecuted—Picked on or made to suffer.

petition—A formal or written statement signed by a number of people.

specter—A ghost or spirit.

supernatural—Beyond the laws of nature or science.

suspects—People who are accused of something.

testify—To make an official statement, as in court.

theory—An idea that has not been proven.

tortured—Hurt or tormented physically and/or mentally.

verdict—A decision made by a jury in a trial.

wizard—A term sometimes used for a male witch.

Timeline

1400s–1600s—Many thousands of so-called witches are put to death in Europe

1604—Britain's Witchcraft Act makes practicing witchcraft a crime punishable by hanging

1620—English colonization of what is now Massachusetts begins

1628—Salem, Massachusetts, is founded by English Puritans

1630—English Puritans establish Boston, Massachusetts

1648—Margaret Jones becomes the first Massachusetts resident put to death for practicing witchcraft

1692—January: Cousins Betty Parris and Abigail Williams of Salem Village appear to be bewitched
February: The Salem witch hunt begins
June: The Salem witch trials and hangings begin with Bridget Bishop
September: The last of nineteen hangings takes place
October: Massachusetts governor William Phips acts to end the Salem witch hunt and trials

1604   *1648*   1692

1693—Governor Phips orders the release of all accused witches still in jail

1776—The United States declares its independence from Britain

1697—Reverend Samuel Parris, blamed by many for the witchcraft hysteria, is kicked out of Salem

1791—The Bill of Rights, protecting rights of accused people and other basic rights, goes into effect

1706—Ann Putnam Jr. publicly apologizes at the Salem Village church for her role in the witch hunt

1992—People commemorate the three hundredth anniversary of the Salem witch hunt and trials

1697   *1706*   *1992*

Further Information

B O O K S

Boraas, Tracey. *The Salem Witch Trials*. Mankato, MN: Capstone Press, 2004.

Burgan, Michael. *The Salem Witch Trials*. Minneapolis, MN: Compass Point Books, 2005.

Orr, Tamra. *The Salem Witch Trials*. San Diego: Blackbirch Press, 2004.

Yolen, Jane, and Heidi Elisabet Yolen Stemple. *The Salem Witch Trials: An Unsolved Mystery from History*. New York: Simon & Schuster, 2004.

W E B S I T E S

This site has information about the Salem witch hunt and trials and life in Salem in 1692:

http://school.discovery.com/schooladventures/salemwitchtrials/

This exciting National Geographic site takes you back to Salem in 1692:

http://www3.nationalgeographic.com/salem/

Check out this account of events in Salem in 1692. There are links to many related topics, including brief biographies of the people involved:

http://www.law.umkc.edu/faculty/projects/ftrials/salem/SALEM.HTM

Visit this site for a brief history of Salem, Massachusetts, including the witch trials period:

http://www.salem.org/17th_Century.asp

Bibliography

Demos, John Putnam. *Entertaining Satan: Witchcraft and the Culture of Early New England.* New York: Oxford University Press, 2004.

Grimassi, Raven. *The Witches' Craft: The Roots of Witchcraft & Magical Transformation.* St. Paul, MN: Llewellyn Publications, 2002.

Hill, Frances. *A Delusion of Satan: The Full Story of the Salem Witch Trials.* Cambridge, MA: Da Capo Press, 2002.

_____.*The Salem Witch Trials Reader.* New York: DaCapo Press, 2000.

Jones, Leslie Ellen. *From Witch to Wicca.* New York: Cold Spring Press, 2004.

Karlsen, Carol F. *The Devil in the Shape of a Woman: Witchcraft in Colonial New England.* New York: Norton, 1998.

Norton, Mary Beth. *In the Devil's Snare: The Salem Witchcraft Crisis of 1692.* New York: Knopf, 2002.

Roach, Marilynne K. *The Salem Witch Trials: A Day-By-Day Chronicle of a Community Under Siege.* New York: Cooper Square Press, 2002.

Russell, Jeffrey Burton. *Witchcraft in the Middle Ages.* Ithaca, NY: Cornell University Press, 1972.

Index

Page numbers in **boldface** are illustrations.

About the Authors

Dennis Fradin is the author of 150 books, some of them written with his wife, Judith Bloom Fradin. Their book for Clarion, *The Power of One: Daisy Bates and the Little Rock Nine,* was named a Golden Kite Honor Book. Another of Dennis's well-known books is *Let It Begin Here! Lexington & Concord: First Battles of the American Revolution,* published by Walker. Other recent books by the Fradins include *Jane Addams: Champion of Democracy* for Clarion and *5,000 Miles to Freedom: Ellen and William Craft's Flight from Slavery* for National Geographic Children's Books. Their current project for National Geographic is the *Witness to Disaster* series about natural disasters. *Turning Points in U.S. History* is Dennis and Judy's first series for Marshall Cavendish Benchmark. The Fradins have three grown children and five grandchildren.